Nihil Obstat: Very Rev. Timothy J. Shea, V.F.

Imprimatur: + Bernard Cardinal Law
September 10, 1992

ISBN 0-8198-0360-X

Copyright © 1992, 1977, by the Daughters of St. Paul
Second edition, 1992

Printed and published in the U.S.A. by St. Paul Books & Media, 50 St. Paul's Avenue, Boston, MA 02130.

St. Paul Books & Media is the publishing house of the Daughters of St. Paul, an international congregation of women religious serving the Church with the communications media.

My Prayerbook

Written and Illustrated
by the Daughters of St. Paul

St. Paul Books & Media

With
my book
I learn to pray.
"To pray"
means
to talk
to God.
I talk to God
and to Jesus.
Jesus is God's Son.

In the morning
I say,
"Hi!"
to Jesus.
I ask God to bless
Mom,
Dad,
me,
and all the people
in the world.
I love you, Jesus.

**Help me
to act the way
you like me to act.**

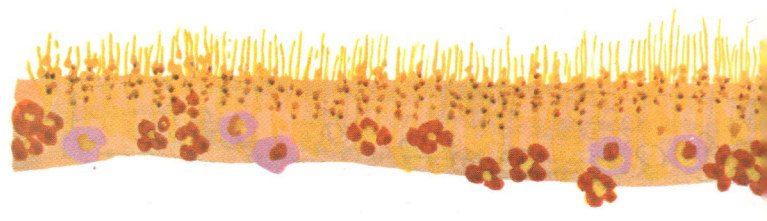

God
made me and
my friends.
God made
the flowers,
the trees,
the birds
and everything.
How good God is!

At night I say,

**Thank you, God,
for Mom, Dad, me,
and everyone else in the
whole world.
Good night, Jesus.**

Jesus has a
Mother.
Her name
is Mary.
**Mary, Mother of
Jesus,
I love you.
Teach me to love Jesus.**

When I play,
I share
my toys
with all my
friends.

In school
I ask Jesus,

**Help me to learn to
read and write.**

"Mom and Dad, I love you very much."

**Jesus,
please take care
of Mom and Dad.**

When I have
a little pain,
I tell Jesus,

**I know you are
with me,
Jesus.**

Before I eat, I say,

**Jesus, please
bless us and the food
we will eat.**

After I eat, I say,

**Jesus, thank you
for the good food
and everything you
give me.
Please give food to
poor people, too.**

Jesus, I want to be
obedient and kind.
I pray
that everyone
in the world
will love You.
Bless the children
all over the world.

When I was baptized,
I became a
child of God
in a special way.
How happy I should be!
My name is _____ .
I received my name
on the day of my
Baptism.
Now, I am part of
God's Family, the Church.

**God, thank you
for making me your child and
keeping me alive and strong.**

When I do something wrong,
I say,
Forgive me, Jesus.

I tell the person I hurt,
"I am sorry."

Jesus tells me to love everybody because we are all children of God.

God made
the sun,
the moon,
and the stars.

God made
water, birds,
and all good
things in the
world.
God made the
first people, too!

God,
you are really good to me.
You gave me
my Mom, Dad,
brothers, sisters and all
my friends.
You give me everything I
need.

Thank you, God!

The Sign of the Cross

**In the name of the Father,
and of the Son,
and of the Holy Spirit.
Amen.**

The Lord's Prayer

Jesus taught us this prayer:

**Our Father who art in heaven,
hallowed be thy name;
thy kingdom come;
thy will be done on earth as it is in heaven.
Give us this day our daily bread;
and forgive us our trespasses
as we forgive those
who trespass against us;
and lead us not into temptation,
but deliver us from evil.
Amen.**

The Hail Mary

**Hail Mary, full of grace!
the Lord is with you;
blessed are you among women,
and blessed is
the fruit of your womb,
Jesus.
Holy Mary, Mother of God,
pray for us sinners now
and at the hour of our death.
Amen.**

Prayer to the Guardian Angel

**Angel sent by God to guide me,
be my light and walk beside me;
be my guardian and protect me;
on the paths of life direct me.**

St. Paul Book & Media Centers

ALASKA
750 West 5th Ave., Anchorage, AK 99501 907-272-8183.

CALIFORNIA
3908 Sepulveda Blvd., Culver City, CA 90230 310-397-8676.
1570 Fifth Ave. (at Cedar Street), San Diego, CA 92101 619-232-1442; 619-232-1443.
46 Geary Street, San Francisco, CA 94108 415-781-5180.

FLORIDA
145 S.W. 107th Ave., Miami, FL 33174 305-559-6715; 305-559-6716.

HAWAII
1143 Bishop Street, Honolulu, HI 96813 808-521-2731.

ILLINOIS
172 North Michigan Ave., Chicago, IL 60601 312-346-4228; 312-346-3240.

LOUISIANA
4403 Veterans Memorial Blvd., Metairie, LA 70006 504-887-7631; 504-887-0113.

MASSACHUSETTS
50 St. Paul's Ave., Jamaica Plain, Boston, MA 02130 617-522-8911.
Rte. 1, 885 Providence Hwy., Dedham, MA 02026 617-326-5385.

MISSOURI
9804 Watson Rd., St. Louis, MO 63126 314-965-3512; 314-965-3571.

NEW JERSEY
561 U.S. Route 1, Wick Plaza, Edison, NJ 08817 908-572-1200.

NEW YORK
150 East 52nd Street, New York, NY 10022 212-754-1110.
78 Fort Place, Staten Island, NY 10301 718-447-5071; 718-447-5086.

OHIO
2105 Ontario Street (at Prospect Ave.), Cleveland, OH 44115 216-621-9427.

PENNSYLVANIA
214 W. DeKalb Pike, King of Prussia, PA 19406 215-337-1882; 215-337-2077.

SOUTH CAROLINA
243 King Street, Charleston, SC 29401 803-577-0175.

TEXAS
114 Main Plaza, San Antonio, TX 78205 210-224-8101.

VIRGINIA
1025 King Street, Alexandria, VA 22314 703-549-3806.

CANADA
3022 Dufferin Street, Toronto, Ontario, Canada M6B 3T5 416-781-9131.